EZ GUITAR
WITH NOTES AND TAB

Favorite Hymns
for EASY GUITAR

T0048257

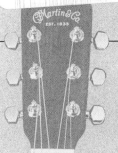

ISBN 978-0-7935-7428-5

HAL•LEONARD®
CORPORATION

7777 W. BLUEMOUND RD. P.O. BOX 13819 MILWAUKEE, WI 53213

Visit Hal Leonard Online at
www.halleonard.com

STRUM AND PICK PATTERNS

This chart contains the suggested strum and pick patterns that are referred to by number at the beginning of each song in this book. The symbols ⊓ and ∨ in the strum patterns refer to down and up strokes, respectively. The letters in the pick patterns indicate which right-hand fingers plays which strings.

p = thumb
i = index finger
m = middle finger
a = ring finger

For example; Pick Pattern 2
is played: thumb - index - middle - ring

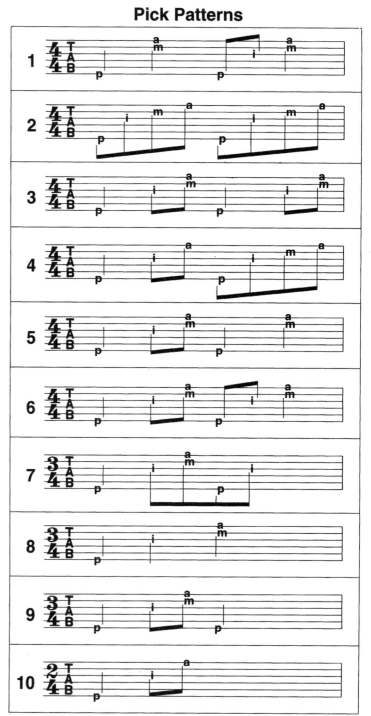

You can use the 3/4 Strum or Pick Patterns in songs written in compound meter (6/8, 9/8, 12/8, etc.).
For example, you can accompany a song in 6/8 by playing the 3/4 pattern twice in each measure.
The 4/4 Strum and Pick Patterns can be used for songs written in cut time (¢) by doubling the note time values in the patterns. Each pattern would therefore last two measures in cut time.

Favorite Hymns for EASY GUITAR

Abide With Me

Words by Henry F. Lyte
Music by W.H. Monk

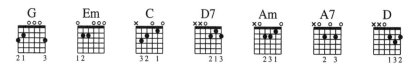

Strum Pattern: 4
Pick Pattern: 5

Chorus

Moderately

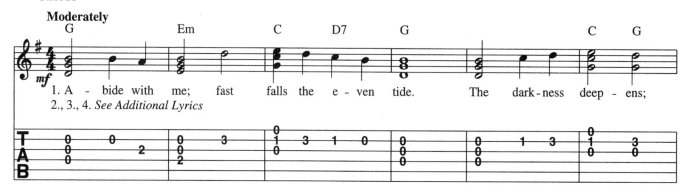

1. A - bide with me; fast falls the e - ven tide. The dark - ness deep - ens;
2., 3., 4. *See Additional Lyrics*

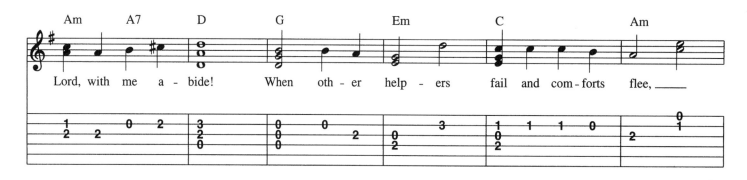

Lord, with me a - bide! When oth - er help - ers fail and com - forts flee, _____

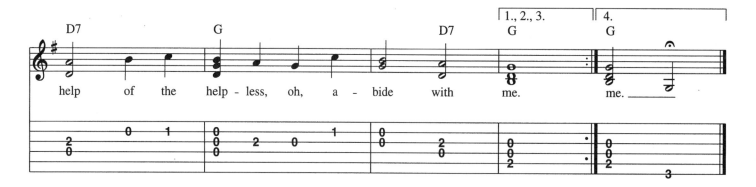

help of the help - less, oh, a - bide with me. me. _____

Additional Lyrics

2. Swift to its close ebbs out life's little day.
Earth's joys grow dim, its glories pass away.
Change and decay in all around I see.
Oh, Thou who changest not, abide with me.

3. I need Thy presence every passing hour;
What but Thy grace can foil the tempter's power?
Who like Thy self, my guide and stay can be?
Through cloud and sunshine, Lord, abide with me.

4. I fear no foe with Thee at hand to bless.
Ills have no weight, and tears no bitterness.
Where is death's sting? Where, grave, Thy victory?
I triumph still if Thou abide with me.

All Hail the Power of Jesus' Name

Traditional

Additional Lyrics

2. Let ev'ry kindred, ev'ry tribe on this terrestrial ball.
   To Him all majesty ascribe and crown Him Lord of all.
   To Him all majesty ascribe and crown Him Lord of all.

3. Oh, that with yonder sacred throng we at His feet may fall.
   We'll join the everlasting song and crown Him Lord of all.
   We'll join the everlasting song and crown Him Lord of all.

All Creatures of Our God and King

Traditional

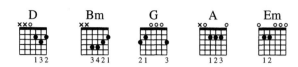

Strum Pattern: 8
Pick Pattern: 8

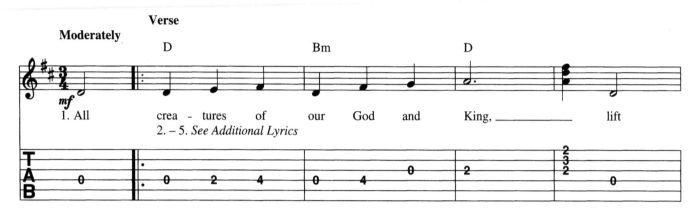

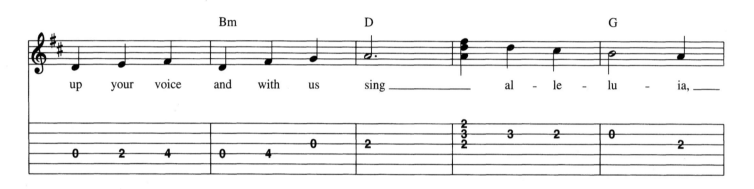

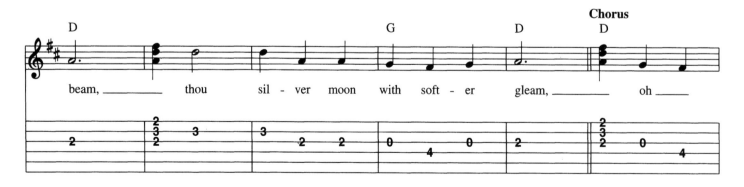

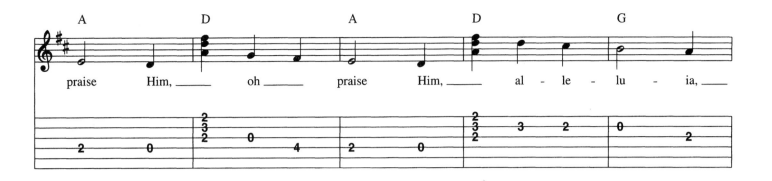

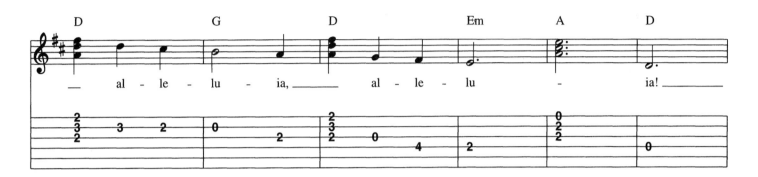

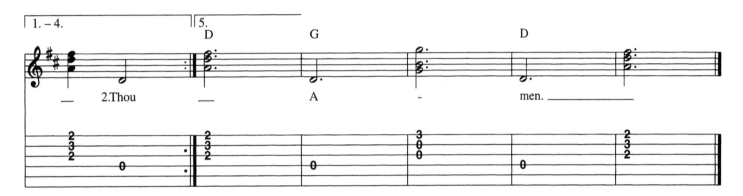

Additional Lyrics

2. Thou rushing wind that art so strong,
   Ye clouds that sail in heav'n along,
   Oh praise Him, alleluia!
   Thou rising morn in praise rejoice,
   Ye lights of evening, find a voice,

3. Thou flowing water, pure and clear,
   Make music for thy Lord to hear,
   Oh praise Him, alleluia!
   Thou fire so masterful and bright,
   That givist man both warmth and light,

4. And all ye men of tender heart,
   Forgiving others, take your part,
   Oh sing ye, alleluia!
   Ye who long pain and sorrow bear,
   Praise God and on Him cast your care,

5. Let all things their Creator bless,
   And worship Him in humbleness,
   Oh praise Him, alleluia!
   Praise, praise the Father, praise the Son,
   And praise the Spirit, three in one,

All Things Bright and Beautiful

Words by Cecil F. Alexander
Traditional Melody

Strum Pattern: 4
Pick Pattern: 4

Additional Lyrics

2. The purple headed mountains, the river running by,
   The sunset and the morning that brightens up the sky.

3. The cold wind in the winter, the pleasant summer sun,
   The ripe fruits in the garden; God made them everyone.

4. God gave us eyes to see them, and lips that we might tell
   How great is God almighty, who has made all things well.

Amazing Grace

Words by John Newton
Traditional American Melody

Strum Pattern: 7
Pick Pattern: 7

Additional Lyrics

2. 'Twas grace that taught my heart to fear,
   And grace my fears relieved.
   How precious did that grace appear
   The hour I first believed.

3. Through many dangers, toils and snares,
   I have already come.
   'Tis grace has brought me safe thus far,
   And grace will lead me home.

4. The Lord has promised good to me,
   His word my hope secures.
   He will my shield and portion be
   As long as life endures.

5. And when this flesh and heart shall fail,
   And mortal life shall cease.
   I shall possess within the veil
   A life of joy and peace.

6. When we've been there ten thousand years,
   Bright shining as the sun.
   We've no less days to sing God's praise
   Than when we first begun.

Be Thou My Vision

Traditional Irish

Strum Pattern: 8
Pick Pattern: 8

Verse
Moderately

1. Be Thou my ___ vi - sion, oh Lord of my heart.
2., 3., 4. *See Additional Lyrics*

Naught be all else to me, save that Thou art. ___

Thou my ___ best ___ thought, __ by day or by night, ___ wak - ing or

sleep - ing, Thy ___ pres - ence my light. A - men.

play 4 times

Additional Lyrics

2. Be Thou my wisdom, and Thou my true word.
   I ever with Thee and Thou with me, Lord.
   Thou my great Father, I Thy true son,
   Thou in me dwelling, and I with Thee one.

3. Riches I heed not, nor man's empty praise.
   Thou mine inheritance, now and always.
   Thou and Thou only, first in my heart,
   High King of heaven, my treasure Thou art.

4. High King of heaven, my victory won.
   May I reach heaven's joys, oh bright heav'n's sun!
   Heart of my own heart, whatever befall,
   Still be my vision, oh Ruler of all.

Beneath the Cross of Jesus

Words by Elizabeth C. Clephane
Music by Frederick C. Maker

Strum Pattern: 3
Pick Pattern: 3

Additional Lyrics

2. Upon the cross of Jesus, mine eye at times can see
The very dying form of One who suffered there for me.
And from my stricken heart, with tears, two wonders I confess:
The wonders of redeeming love and my unworthiness.

Blessed Assurance

Lyrics by Fanny Crosby and Van Alstyne
Music by Phoebe P. Knapp

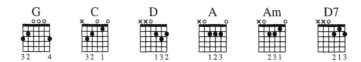

Strum Pattern: 8
Pick Pattern: 8

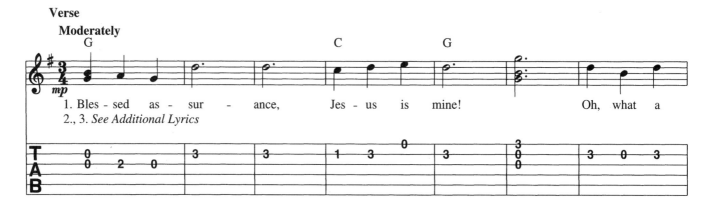

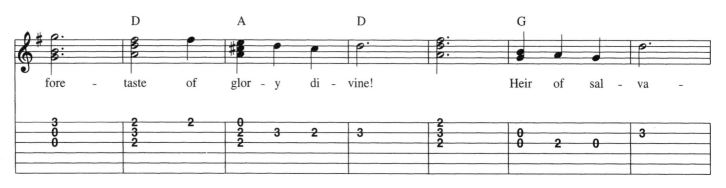

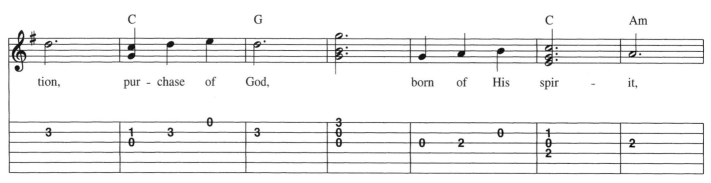

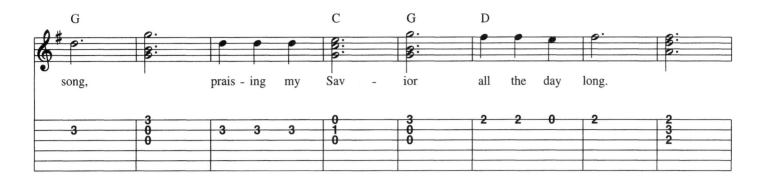

song, prais - ing my Sav - ior all the day long.

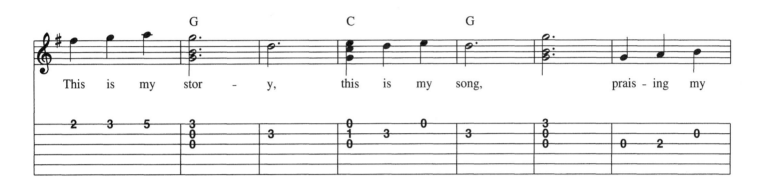

This is my stor - y, this is my song, prais - ing my

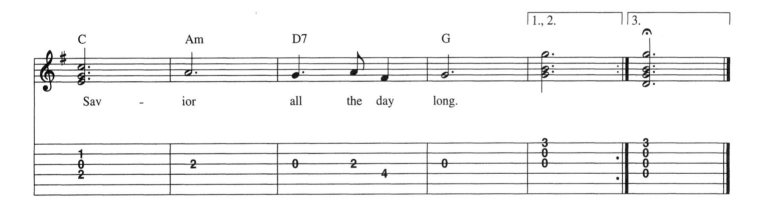

Sav - ior all the day long.

Additional Lyrics

2. Perfect submission, perfect delight,
   Visions of rapture now burst on my sight.
   Angels descending, bring from above
   Echoes of mercy, whispers of love.

3. Perfect submission, all is at rest.
   I in my Savior am happy and blest.
   Watching and waiting, looking above,
   Filled with His goodness, lost in His love.

Breathe on Me, Breath of God

Words by Edwin Hatch
Music by Robert Jackson

Strum Pattern: 8
Pick Pattern: 8

Chorus
Moderately

1. Breathe on me, breath of God. Fill me with life a-
2., 3., 4. *See Additional Lyrics*

new, that I may love what dost Thou love and

do _____ what Thou wouldst do. ty.

Additional Lyrics

2. Breathe on me, breath of God,
   Until my heart is pure,
   Until with Thee, I will one will,
   To do and to endure.

3. Breathe on me, breath of God,
   Till I am wholly Thine,
   Until this earthly part of me
   Glows with Thy fire divine.

4. Breathe on me, breath of God,
   So shall I never die,
   But live with Thee, the perfect life
   Of thine eternity.

The Church's One Foundation

Words by Samuel Stone
Music by Samuel Wesley

Strum Pattern: 4
Pick Pattern: 1

Additional Lyrics

2. Elect from ev'ry nation, yet one o'er all the earth.
   Her charter of salvation, one Lord, one faith, one birth.
   One holy name she blesses, partakes one holy food,
   And to one hope she presses, with ev'ry grace endued.

3. 'Mid toil and tribulation, and tumult of her war,
   She waits the consumation of peace forevermore.
   Till with the vision glorious, her longing eyes are blest,
   And the great church victorious shall be the church at rest.

Close to Thee

Words by Fanny J. Crosby
Music by Silas J. Vail

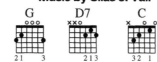

Strum Pattern: 8
Pick Pattern: 8

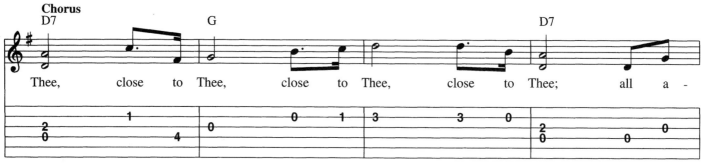

Additional Lyrics

2. Not for ease or worldly pleasure,
Nor for fame my prayer shall be;
Gladly will I toil and suffer,
Only let me walk with Thee.

Chorus 2. Close to Thee, close to Thee,
Close to Thee, close to Thee;
Gladly will I toil and suffer,
Only let me walk with Thee.

3. Lead me through the vail of shadows,
Bear me o'er life's fitful sea;
Then the gate of life eternal,
May I enter, Lord, with Thee.

Chorus 3. Close to Thee, close to Thee,
Close to Thee, close to Thee;
Then the gate of life eternal,
May I enter, Lord, with Thee.

Come, Thou Almighty King

Anonymous Text
Music by Felice de Giardini

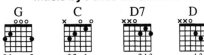

Strum Pattern: 8
Pick Pattern: 8

Verse
Moderately

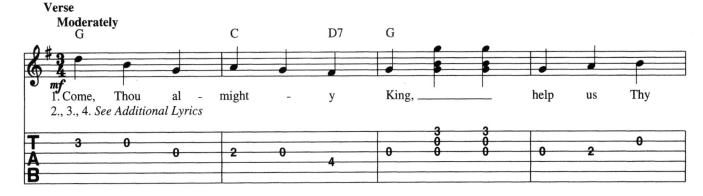

1. Come, Thou al-might-y King, _____ help us Thy
2., 3., 4. *See Additional Lyrics*

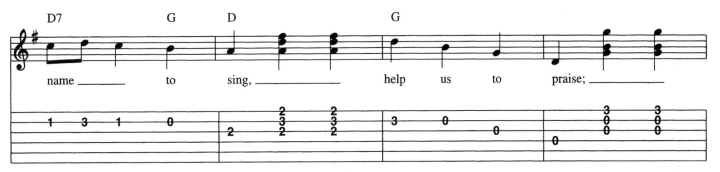

name _____ to sing, _____ help us to praise; _____

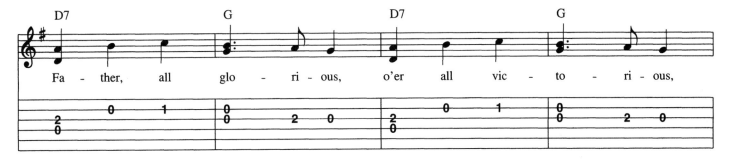

Fa-ther, all glo-ri-ous, o'er all vic-to-ri-ous,

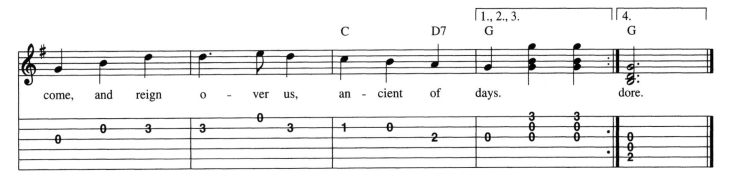

come, and reign o-ver us, an-cient of days. dore.

Additional Lyrics

2. Come, Thou incarnate Word,
Gird on Thy mighty sword;
Our pray'r attend;
Come, and Thy people bless,
And give Thy word success,
Spirit of holiness,
On us descend.

3. Come, holy Comforter!
Thy sacred witness bear,
In this glad hour;
Thou who almighty art,
Now rule in ev'ry heart,
And ne'er from us depart,
Spirit of pow'r!

4. To the great One in Three,
The highest praises be,
Hence ever more!
His sov'reign majesty
May we in glory see,
And to eternity
Love and adore.

Come Christians Join to Sing

Words by Christian Henry Bateman
Traditional Melody

Strum Pattern: 2
Pick Pattern: 2

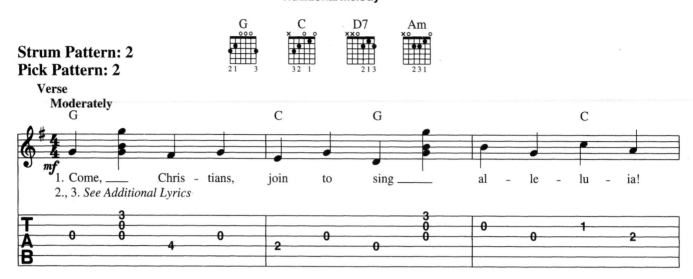

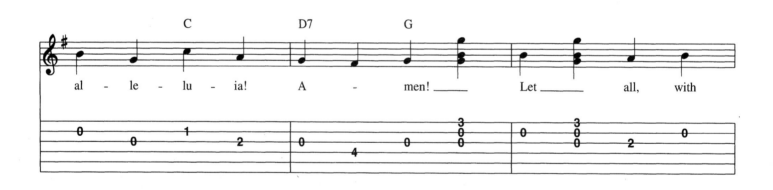

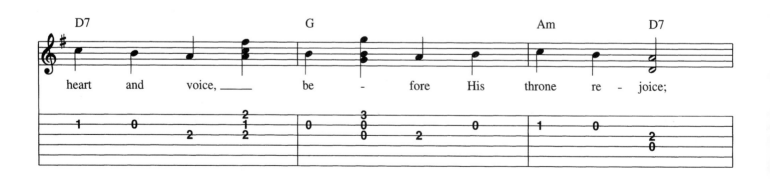

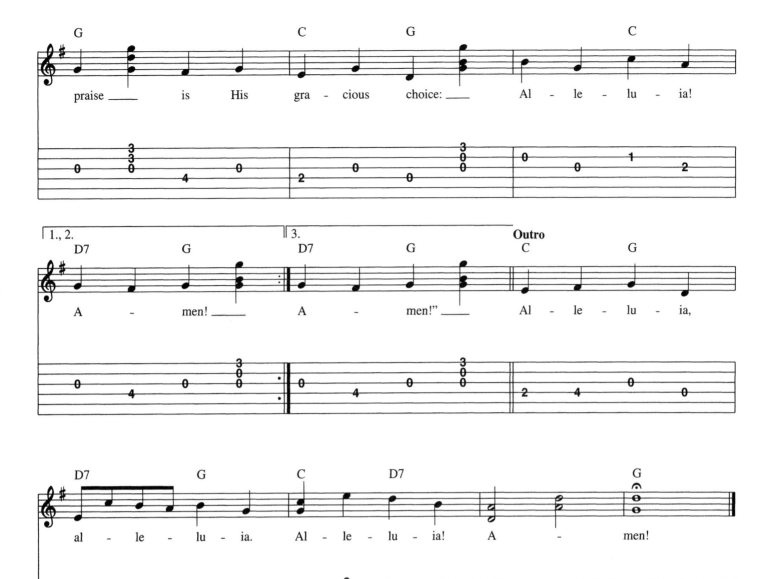

Additional Lyrics

2. Come, lift your hearts on high,
   Alleluia! Amen!
   Let praises fill the sky;
   Alleluia! Amen!
   He is our guide and friend;
   To us He'll condescend;
   His love shall never end:
   Alleluia! Amen!

3. Praise yet our Christ again,
   Alleluia! Amen!
   Life shall not end the strain;
   Alleluia! Amen!
   On heaven's blissful shore
   His goodness we'll adore,
   Singing forevermore,
   "Alleluia! Amen!"

Come, Thou Fount of Every Blessing

Words by Robert Robinson
Traditional Music compiled by Wyeth

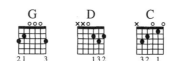

Strum Pattern: 8
Pick Pattern: 8

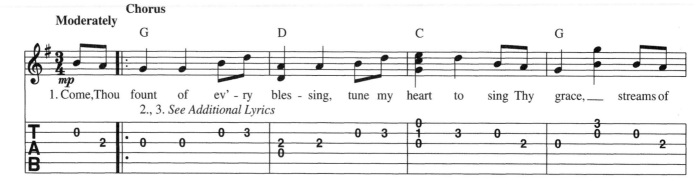

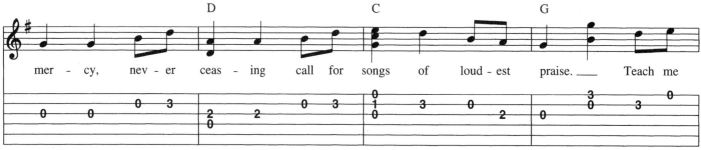

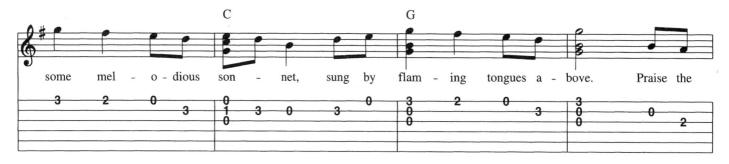

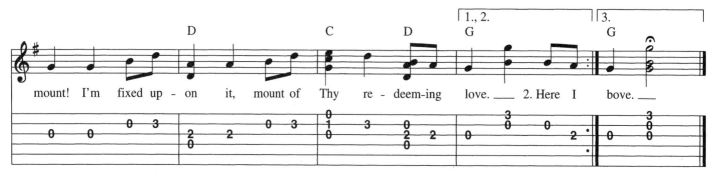

Additional Lyrics

2. Here I raise mine Ebenezer,
   Hither by Thy help I'm come.
   And I hope, by Thy good pleasure,
   Safely to arrive at home.
   Jesus sought me when a stranger,
   Wand'ring from the fold of God;
   He, to rescue me from danger,
   Interposed His precious blood.

3. Oh, to grace how great a debtor
   Daily I'm constrained to be!
   Let Thy grace, Lord, like a fetter,
   Bind my wand'ring heart to Thee.
   Prone to wander, Lord I feel it,
   Prone to leave the God I love;
   Here's my heart, Lord, take and seal it,
   Seal it for Thy courts above.

Fairest Lord Jesus

Words for Stanza 4 by Joseph August Seiss
Music by Schlesische Volkslieder
Arranged by Richard Storrs Willis

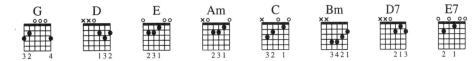

Strum Pattern: 4
Pick Pattern: 4

Chorus

Slowly

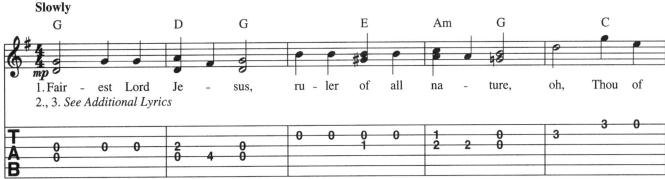

1. Fair - est Lord Je - sus, ru - ler of all na - ture, oh, Thou of
2., 3. *See Additional Lyrics*

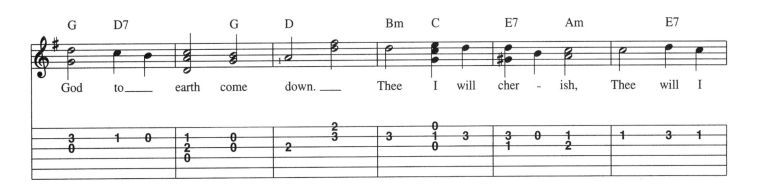

God to___ earth come down. ___ Thee I will cher - ish, Thee will I

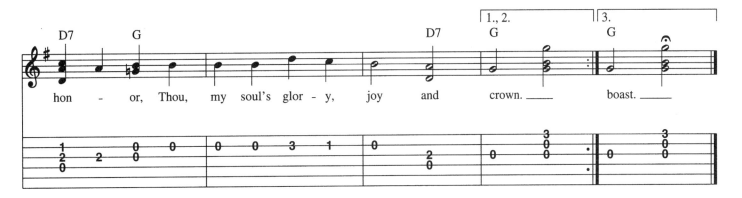

hon - or, Thou, my soul's glor - y, joy and crown. ___ boast. ___

Additional Lyrics

2. Fairest are the meadows, fairer still the woodlands,
   Robed in the blooming garb of spring.
   Jesus is fairer, Jesus is purer,
   Who makes the woeful heart to sing.

3. Fair is the sunshine, fairer still the moonlight,
   And the twinkling, starry host.
   Jesus shines brighter, Jesus shines purer
   Than all the angels heaven can boast.

For the Beauty of the Earth

Text by Folliot S. Pierpoint
Music by Conrad Kocher

Strum Pattern: 4
Pick Pattern: 3

Additional Lyrics

2. For the beauty of each hour
   Of the day and of the night,
   Hill and vale, and tree and flower,
   Sun and moon and stars of light.

4. For the joy of human love,
   Brother, sister, parent, child,
   Friends on earth and friends above,
   For all gentle thoughts and mild.

6. For Thy self, best Gift Divine,
   To the world so freely given,
   For that great, great love of Thine,
   Peace on earth and joy in heaven.

3. For the joy of ear and eye,
   For the heart and mind's delight,
   For the mystic harmony
   Linking sense to sound and sight.

5. For Thy church that evermore
   Lifteth holy hands above,
   Offering upon every shore
   Her pure sacrifice of love.

Optional Chorus for Holy Communion

Christ, our God, to Thee we raise
This our sacrifice of praise.

God of Grace and God of Glory

Text by Harry Emerson Fosdick
Music by John Hughes

Additional Lyrics

2. Lo! The hosts of evil round us
   Scorn Thy Christ, assail His ways!
   From the fears that long have bound us,
   Free our hearts to faith and praise.
   Grant us wisdom, grant us courage,
   For the living of these days,
   For the living of these days.

3. Cure Thy children's warring madness,
   Bend our pride to Thy control.
   Shame our wanton, selfish gladness,
   Rich in things and poor in soul.
   Grant us wisdom, grant us courage,
   Lest we miss Thy Kingdom's goal,
   Lest we miss Thy Kingdom's goal.

4. Set our feet on lofty places,
   Gird our lives that they may be
   Armored with all Christ–like graces
   In the fight to set men free.
   Grant us wisdom, grant us courage,
   That we fail not man nor Thee,
   That we fail not man nor Thee.

He Hideth My Soul

Words by Fanny J. Crosby
Music by William J. Kirkpatrick

Strum Pattern: 8, 9
Pick Pattern: 8, 9

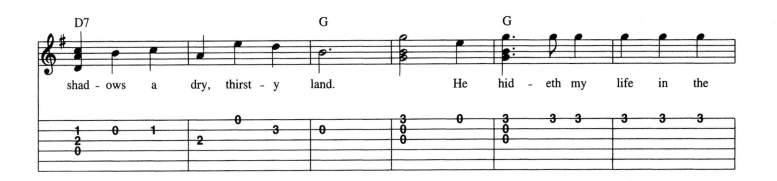

shad - ows   a   dry, thirst - y   land.   He   hid – eth my   life   in   the

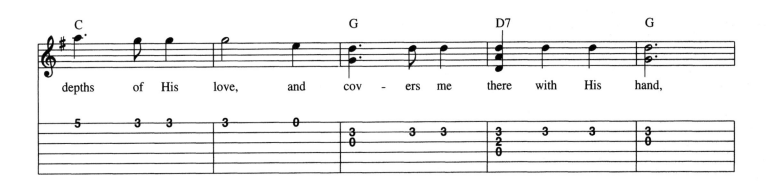

depths   of   His   love,   and   cov   –   ers   me   there   with   His   hand,

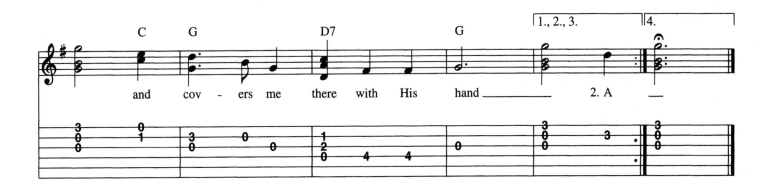

and   cov   –   ers   me   there   with   His   hand _____   2. A _____

Additional Lyrics

2. A wonderful Savior is Jesus my Lord,
   He taketh my burden away.
   He holdeth me up and I shall not be moved.
   He giveth me strength as my day.

3. With numberless blessings, each moment He crowns
   And filled with His fullness divine,
   I sing in my rapture, oh glory to God
   For such a Redeemer as mine!

4. When clothed in His brightness, transported I rise
   To meet Him in clouds of the sky.
   His perfect salvation, His wonderful love,
   I'll shout with the millions on high.

Holy, Holy, Holy! Lord God Almighty

Text by Reginald Heber
Music by John B. Dykes

Strum Pattern: 3
Pick Pattern: 3

Verse
Joyfully

1.Ho - ly, ho - ly, ho - ly! _____ Lord _____ God Al - might - y!
2., 3., 4. *See Additional Lyrics*

Ear - ly in the morn - ing our songs shall rise to Thee. _____

Ho - ly, ho - ly, ho - ly! _____ Mer - ci - ful and might - y! _____

God _____ in three per - sons, bless - ed Trin - i - ty. _____ ty. _____

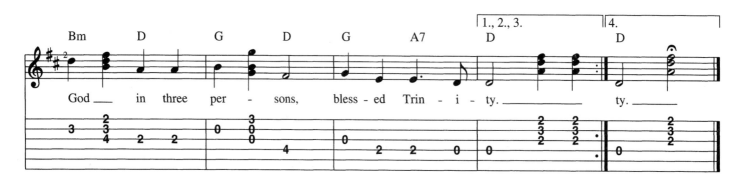

Additional Lyrics

2. Holy, holy, holy! All the saints adore Thee.
   Casting down their golden crowns around the glassy sea.
   Cherubim and seraphim falling down before Thee,
   Which wert, and art, and evermore shall be.

3. Holy, holy, holy! Through the darkness hide Thee.
   Through the eye of sinful man Thy glory may not see.
   Only Thou art holy; there is none beside Thee,
   Perfect in power, in love and purity.

4. Holy, holy, holy! Lord God Almighty!
   All Thy works shall praise Thy name in earth and sky and sea.
   Holy, holy, holy! Merciful and mighty!
   God in three persons, blessed Trinity.

How Firm a Foundation

Traditional Text compiled by John Rippon
Traditional Music compiled by Joseph Funk

Strum Pattern: 2
Pick Pattern: 4

Additional Lyrics

2. "Fear not, I am with thee, oh be not dismayed,
For I am thy God and will still give thee aid.
I'll strengthen thee, help thee and cause thee to stand,
Upheld by My righteous, ominipotent hand."

3. "When through the deep waters I call thee to go,
The rivers of sorrow shall not overflow;
For I will be near thee, thy troubles to bless,
And sanctify to thee thy deepest distress."

4. "When through fiery trials, thy pathway shall lie,
My grace, all sufficient, shall be thy supply.
The flame shall not hurt thee; I only design
Thy dross to consume and thy gold to refine."

I Know Whom I Have Believed

Traditional Hymn

Strum Pattern: 6
Pick Pattern: 6

Additional Lyrics

2. I know not how the Spirit moves,
Convincing men of sin,
Revealing Jesus thru the Word,
Creating faith in Him.

3. I know not what of good or ill
May be reserved for me,
Of weary ways or golden days,
Before His face I see.

4. I know not when my Lord may come,
At night of noonday fair,
Nor if I'll walk the vale* with Him,
Or meet Him in the air.

*Valley of Death

I Love Thy Kingdom, Lord

Words by Tim Dwight
Music by Aaron Williams

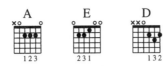

Strum Pattern: 4
Pick Pattern: 4

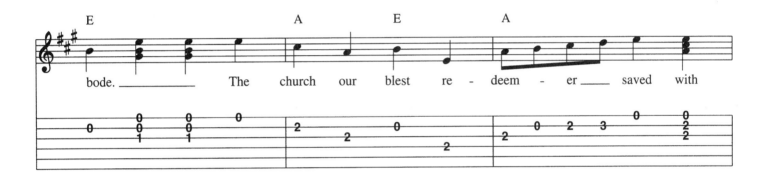

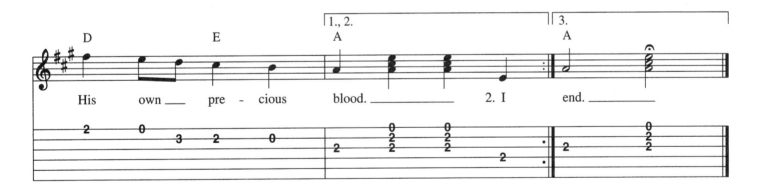

Additional Lyrics

2. I love Thy church, oh, God!
   Her walls before Thee stand,
   Dear as the apple of Thine eye,
   And graven on Thy land.

3. For her my tears shall fall,
   For her my prayers ascend.
   To her my cares and toils be giv'n,
   Till toils and cares shall end.

I Love to Tell the Story

By K. Hankey and W.G. Fischer

Strum Pattern: 4
Pick Pattern: 4

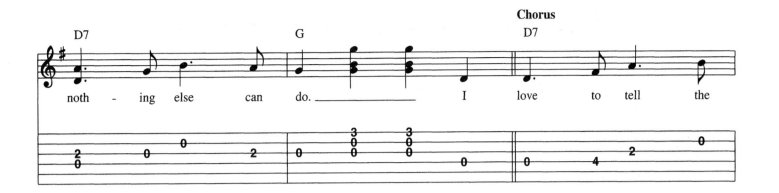

noth - ing else can do. _____ I love to tell the

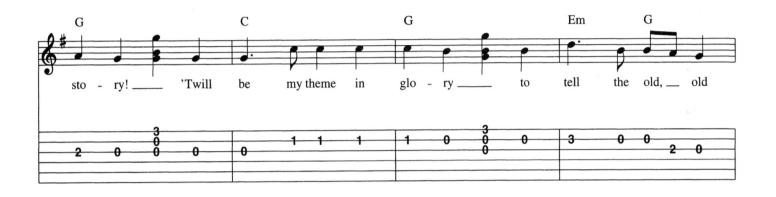

sto - ry! _____ 'Twill be my theme in glo - ry _____ to tell the old, __ old

sto - ry _____ of Je - sus and His love. _____ 2. I love. _____

Additional Lyrics

2. I love to tell the story; more wonderful it seems
   Than all the golden fancies of all our golden dreams.
   I love to tell the story; it did so much for me,
   And that is just the reason I tell it now to thee.

3. I love to tell the story 'tis pleasant to repeat
   What seems each time I tell it, more wonderfully sweet.
   I love to tell the story for some have never heard
   The message of salvation from God's own holy word.

4. I love to tell the story; for those who know it best
   Seem hungering and thirsting to hear it like the rest.
   And when, in scenes of glory, I sing the new, new song,
   'Twill be the old, old story that I have loved so long.

I've Got Peace Like a River

Traditional

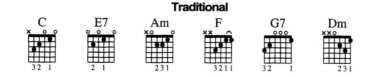

Strum Pattern: 3
Pick Pattern: 3

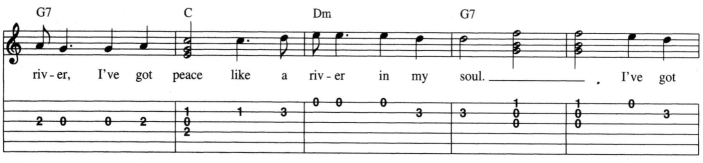

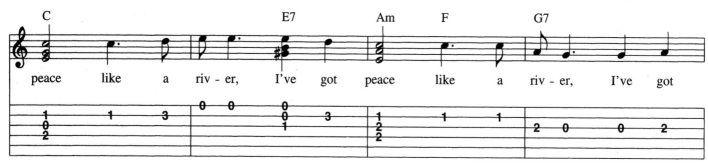

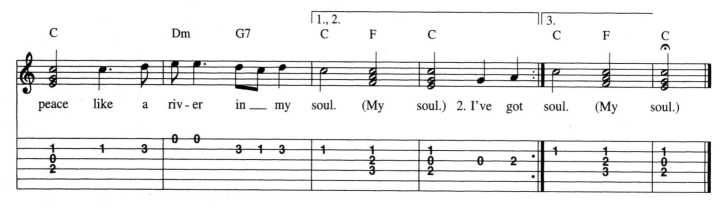

Additional Lyrics

2. I've got love like an ocean,
   I've got love like an ocean,
   I've got love like an ocean in my soul.
   I've got love like an ocean,
   I've got love like an ocean,
   I've got love like an ocean in my soul. (My soul.)

3. I've got joy like a fountain,
   I've got joy like a fountain,
   I've got joy like a fountain in my soul.
   I've got joy like a fountain,
   I've got joy like a fountain,
   I've got joy like a fountain in my soul. (My soul.)

Immortal, Invisible

Words by Walter Chalmers Smith
Traditional Music

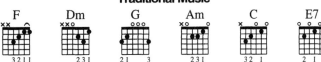

Strum Pattern: 8
Pick Pattern: 8

Additional Lyrics

2. Unresting, unhasting, and silent as light,
   Nor wanting, nor wasting, Thou rulest in might.
   Thy justice like mountains high soaring above
   Thy clouds, which are fountains of goodness and love.

3. To all, life Thou givest, to both great and small,
   In all life Thou livest, the true life of all.
   We blossom and flourish as leaves on the tree,
   And wither and perish but naught changeth Thee.

4. Great Father of glory, pure Father of light,
   Thine angels adore Thee, all veiling their sight.
   All praise we would render, Oh help us to see,
   'Tis only the splendor of light hideth Thee.

In the Garden

Words and Music by C. Austin Miles

Strum Pattern: 8, 9
Pick Pattern: 8, 9

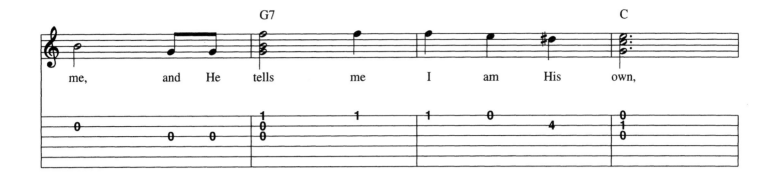

G7 · · · · · · · C

me, and He tells me I am His own,

E7 Am D7

and the joy we share as we tar - ry there, none

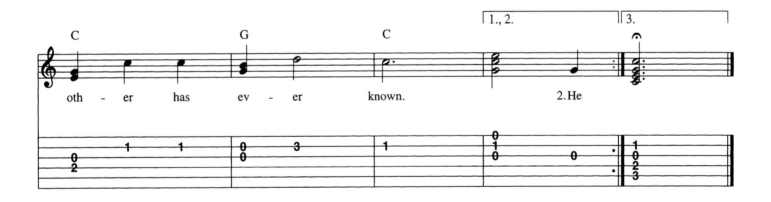

C G C 1., 2. 3.

oth - er has ev - er known. 2. He

Additional Lyrics

2. He speaks, and the sound of His voice
   Is so sweet the birds hush their singing,
   And the melody that He gave to me
   Within my heart is ringing.

3. I'd stay in the garden with Him,
   Though the night around me be falling.
   But He bids me go through the voice of woe;
   His voice to me is calling.

It Is Well With My Soul

Text by Horatio G. Spafford
Music by Philip P. Bliss

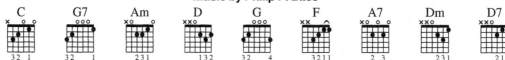

Strum Pattern: 2
Pick Pattern: 2

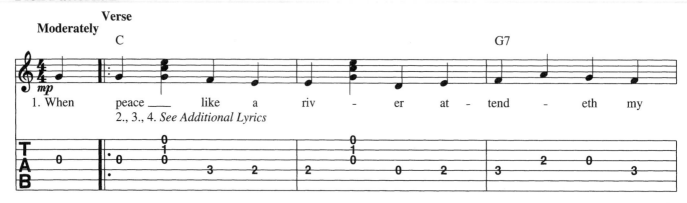

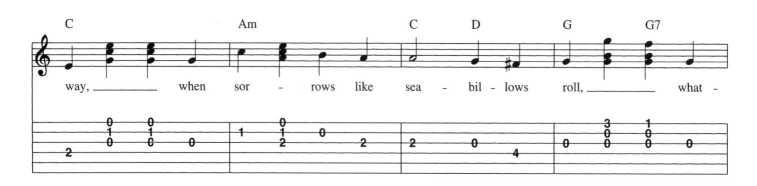

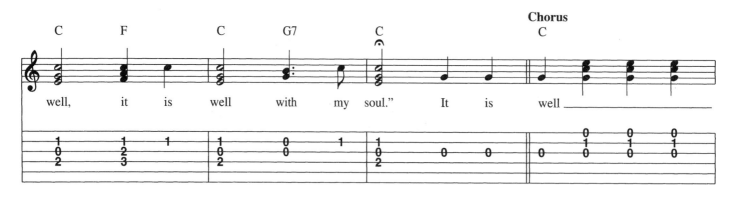

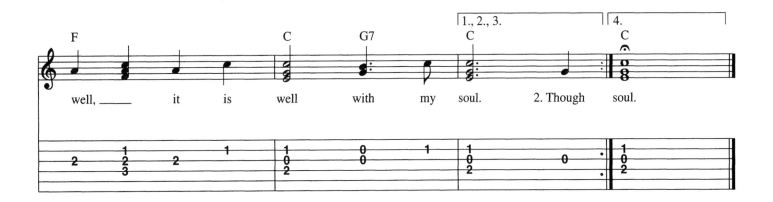

Additional Lyrics

2. Though Satan should buffet, tho' trials should come,
   Let this blest assurance control,
   That Christ has regarded my helpless estate,
   And hath shed His own blood for my soul.

3. My sin oh, the bliss of this glorious thought,
   My sin not in part but the whole,
   Is nailed to the cross and I bear it no more,
   Praise the Lord, praise the Lord, oh my soul!

4. And, Lord, haste the day when the faith shall be sight,
   The clouds be rolled back as a scroll,
   The trump shall resound and the Lord shall descend,
   Even so it is well with my soul.

Jacob's Ladder

African-American Spiritual

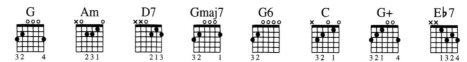

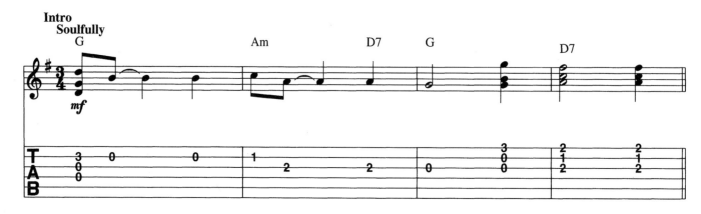

Strum Pattern: 8
Pick Pattern: 8

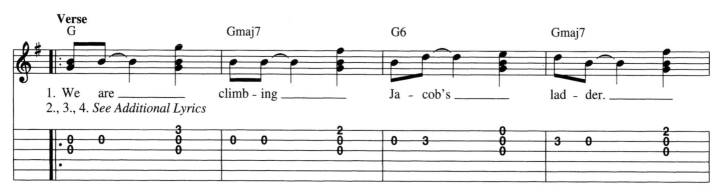

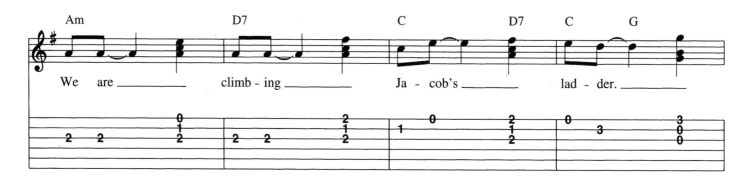

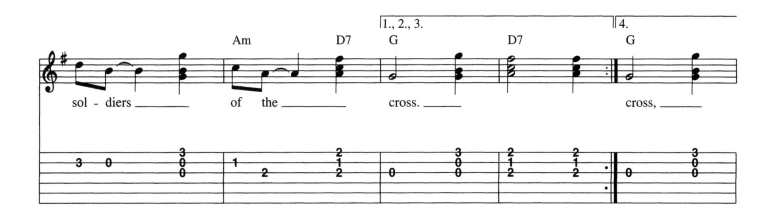

sol - diers _____ of the _____ cross. _____ cross, _____

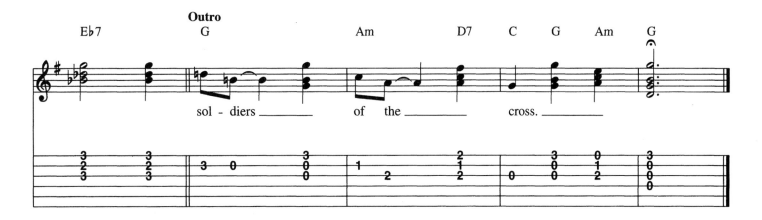

Outro

sol - diers _____ of the _____ cross. _____

Additional Lyrics

2. Ev'ry round goes higher, higher.
   Ev'ry round goes higher, higher.
   Ev'ry round goes higher, higher,
   Soldiers of the cross.

3. We are climbing higher, higher.
   We are climbing higher, higher.
   We are climbing higher, higher,
   Soldiers of the cross.

4. If you love Him, why not serve Him?
   If you love Him, why not serve Him?
   If you love Him, why not serve Him?
   Soldiers of the cross,

Joyful, Joyful We Adore Thee

Words by Henry van Dyke
Music by Ludwig Van Beethoven, melody from Ninth Symphony
Adapted by Edward Hodges

Strum Pattern: 3
Pick Pattern: 4

Additional Lyrics

2. All Thy works with joy surround Thee,
   Earth and heaven reflect Thy rays.
   Stars and angels sing around Thee,
   Center of unbroken praise.
   Field and forest, vale and mountain,
   Flowery meadow, flashing sea,
   Chanting bird and flowing fountain,
   Call us to rejoice in Thee.

3. Mortals, join the happy chorus
   Which the morning stars began.
   Love divine is reigning o'er us,
   Joining all in heaven's plan.
   Ever singing, march we onward,
   Victors in the midst of strife.
   Joyful music leads us sunward.
   In the triumph song of life.

Let Us Break Bread Together

African-American Spiritual

Strum Pattern: 3
Pick Pattern: 3

1. Let us break bread to-geth-er on our knees, (on our

2., 3. *See Additional Lyircs*

knees.) Let us break bread to-geth-er on our knees, (on our

knees.) When I fall on my knees with my face to the ris-ing sun, oh

Lord, have mer-cy on me, (on me.) 2. Let us me.)

Additional Lyrics

2. Let us drink the cup together on our knees,
   (On our knees.)
   Let us drink the cup together on our knees,
   (On our knees.)

3. Let us praise God together on our knees,
   (On our knees,)
   Let us praise God together on our knees,
   (On our knees.)

Like a River Glorious

Traditional

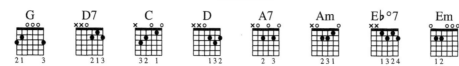

Strum Pattern: 4
Pick Pattern: 4

Verse
Moderately

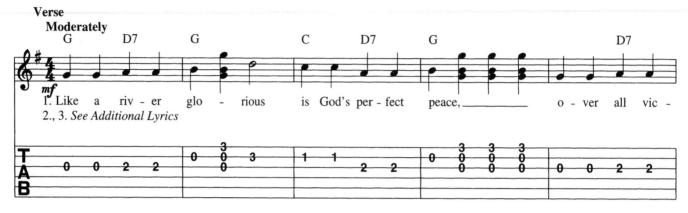

Lyrics:
1. Like a riv-er glo-rious is God's per-fect peace,_____ o-ver all vic-
2., 3. *See Additional Lyrics*

to-rious_ in its bright in-crease._____ Per-fect, yet it flow-eth,__ full-er ev-'ry

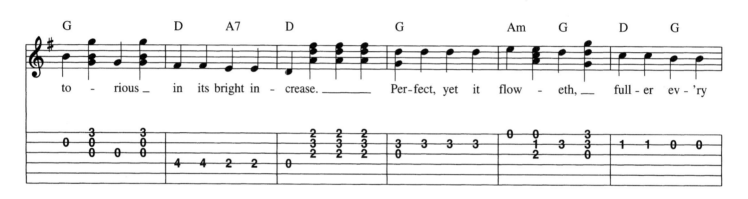

day._____ Per-fect, yet it grow-eth, deep-er all the way._____ true.___

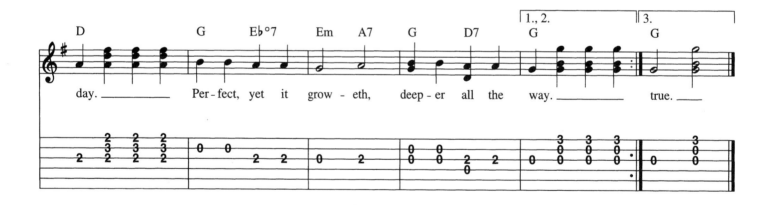

Additional Lyrics

2. Hidden in the hollow of His blessed hand,
Never foe can follow, never traitor stand.
Not a surge of worry, not a shade of care,
Not a blast of hurry touch the Spirit there.

3. Ev'ry joy or trial falleth from above,
Traced upon our dial by the sun of love.
We must trust him fully, all for us to do.
They who trust Him wholly find Him wholly true.

My Faith Has Found a Resting Place

Traditional

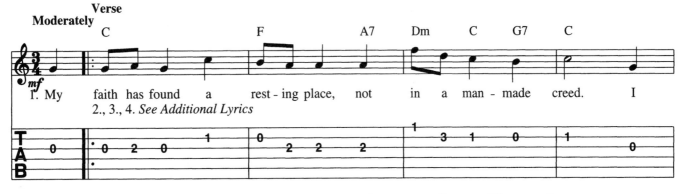

Strum Pattern: 8
Pick Pattern: 8

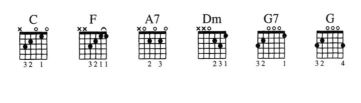

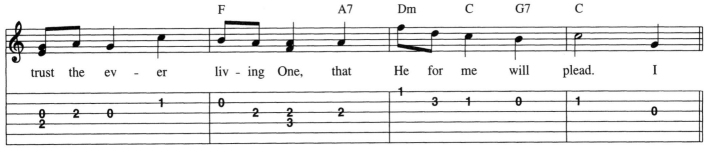

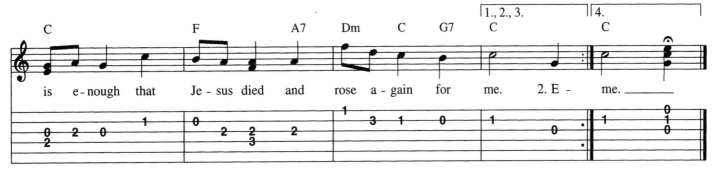

Additional Lyrics

2. Enough for me that Jesus saves,
   This ends my fear and doubt.
   A sinful soul I come to Him,
   He will not cast me out.

3. My soul is resting on the Word,
   The living Word of God.
   Salvation in my Savior's name,
   Salvation through His blood.

4. The great Physician heals the sick,
   The lost He came to save;
   For me His precious blood He shed,
   For me His life He gave.

My Faith Looks up to Thee

Traditional

Strum Pattern: 3
Pick Pattern: 3

Additional Lyrics

2. When ends life's transient dream,
   When death's cold, sullen stream
   Shall o'er me roll,
   Blest Saviour, then, in love,
   Fear and distrust remove.
   Oh bear me safe above,
   A ransomed soul! Amen.

3. While life's dark maze I tread,
   And griefs around me spread,
   Be Thou my guide.
   Bid darkness turn to day,
   Wipe sorrow's tears away,
   Nor let me ever stray
   From Thee aside. Amen.

4. May Thy rich grace impart
   Strength to my fainting heart,
   My zeal inspire.
   As Thou has died for me,
   Oh may my love to Thee,
   Pure, warm, and changeless be,
   A living fire! Amen.

My Jesus, I Love Thee

Text by William R. Featherstone
Music by Adoniram J. Gordon

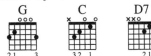

Strum Pattern: 3
Pick Pattern: 3

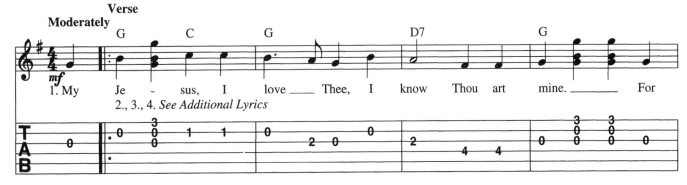

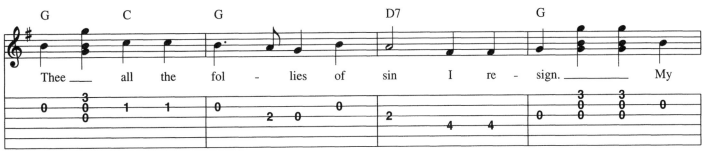

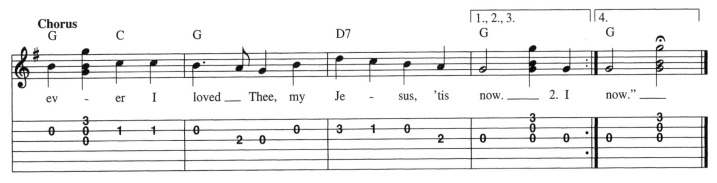

Additional Lyrics

2. I love Thee because Thou hast first loved me
   And purchased my pardon on Calvary's tree.
   I love Thee for wearing the thorns on Thy brow.

3. I'll love Thee in life, I will love Thee in death,
   And praise Thee as long as Thou lendest me breath.
   And say when the death dew lies cold on my brow, "If…

4. In mansions of glory and endless delight,
   I'll ever adore Thee in heaven so bright.
   I'll sing with the glittering crown on my brow, "If…

Near the Cross

Words by Fanny Crosby
Music by William H. Doane

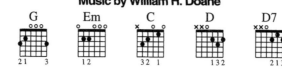

Strum Pattern: 8
Pick Pattern: 8

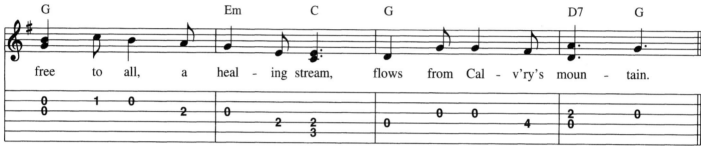

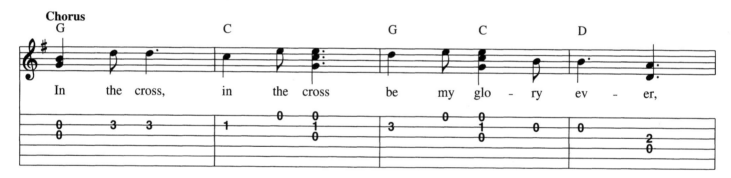

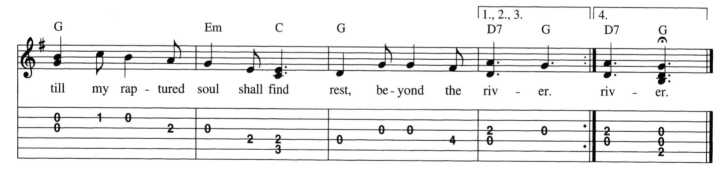

Additional Lyrics

2. Near the cross, a trembling soul,
   Love and mercy found me.
   There the bright and morning star
   Sheds its beams around me.

3. Near the cross! Oh Lamb of God,
   Bring its scenes before me.
   Help my walk from day to day,
   With its shadows o'er me.

4. Near the cross I'll watch and wait,
   Hoping, trusting ever,
   Till I reach the golden strand
   Just beyond the river.

Now Thank We All Our God

German Words by Martin Rinckart
English Translation by Catherine Winkworth
Tune by Ahasverus Fritsch
Setting by Johann Sebastian Bach (from CANTATA 129)

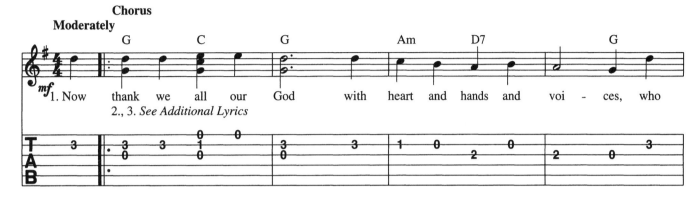

Strum Pattern: 3
Pick Pattern: 4

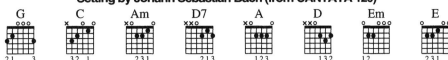

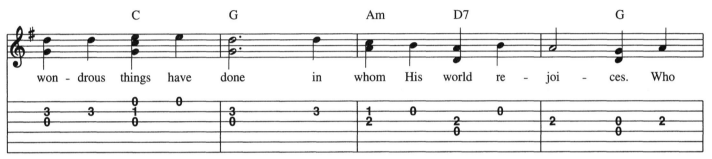

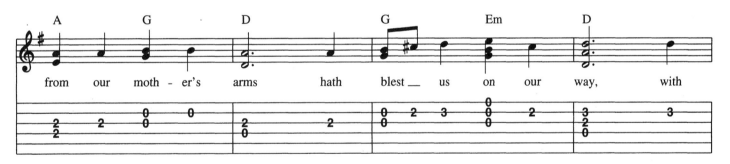

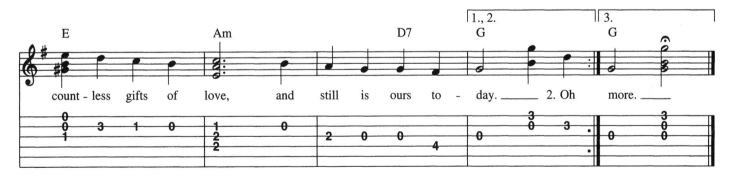

Additional Lyrics

2. Oh may this bounteous God through all our life be near us,
   With ever joyful hearts and blessed peace to cheer us.
   And keep us in His grace and guide us when perplexed,
   And free us from all ills in this world and the next.

3. All praise and thanks to God, the Father now be given,
   The Son and Him who reigns with them in highest heaven.
   The one eternal God, whom earth and heaven adore,
   For thus it was, is now and shall be evermore.

O For a Thousand Tongues to Sing

Text by Charles Wesley
Music by Carl G. Glaser

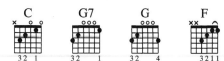

Strum Pattern: 8
Pick Pattern: 8

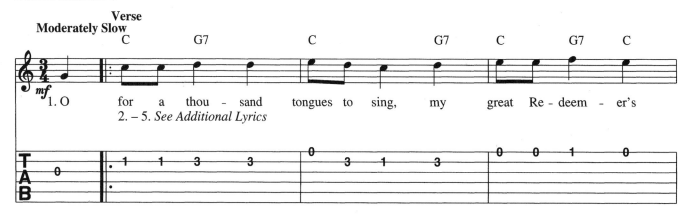

1. O for a thou-sand tongues to sing, my great Re-deem-er's
2. – 5. *See Additional Lyrics*

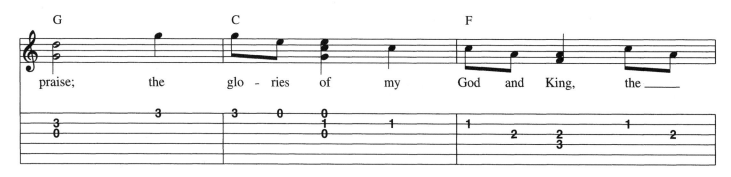

praise; the glo-ries of my God and King, the _____

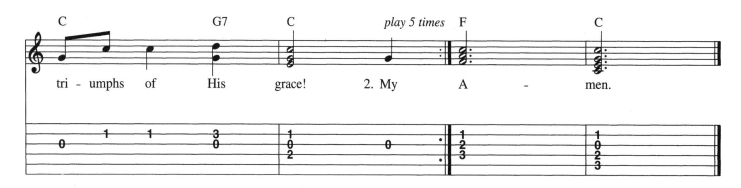

tri-umphs of His grace! 2. My A - men.

Additional Lyrics

2. My gracious Master and my God,
   Assist me to proclaim,
   To spread through all the earth abroad
   The honors of Thy name.

3. Jesus! The name that charms our fears,
   That bids our sorrows cease,
   'Tis music in the sinner's ears,
   'Tis life and health and peace.

4. He breaks the pow'r of canceled sin,
   He sets the prisoner free;
   His blood can make the foulest clean,
   His blood availed for me.

5. Hear Him, ye deaf, His praise, ye dumb,
   Your loosened tongues employ;
   Ye blind, behold your Savior come,
   And leap, ye lame, for joy!

O Love That Wilt Not Let Me Go

Traditional

Strum Pattern: 3
Pick Pattern: 4

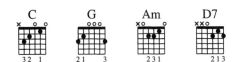

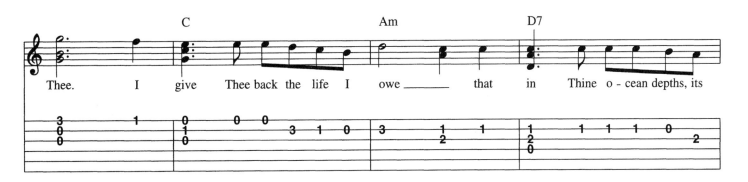

1. O Love__ that wilt not let me go, I rest my wear - y soul in
2., 3., 4. *See Additional Lyrics*

Thee. I give Thee back the life I owe __ that in Thine o - cean depths, its

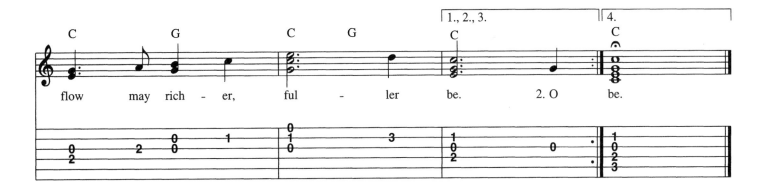

flow may rich - er, ful - ler be. 2. O be.

Additional Lyrics

2. I light foll'west all my way,
   I yield my flick'ring torch to Thee.
   My heart restores its borrowed ray,
   That in Thy sunshine's glow its day
   May brighter, fairer be.

3. O joy that seekest me thro' pain,
   I cannot close my heart to Thee.
   I trace the rainbow thro' the rain,
   And feel the promise is not vain
   That morn shall tearless be.

4. O cross that liftest up my head,
   I dare not ask to hide from Thee.
   I lay in dust, life's glory dead,
   And from the ground there, blossoms red,
   Life that shall endless be.

Pass Me Not, O Gentle Savior

Traditional

Strum Pattern: 5
Pick Pattern: 1

Additional Lyrics

2. Let me at a throne of mercy,
   Find a sweet relief;
   Kneeling there in deep contrition
   Help my unbelief.

3. Trusting only in Thy merit,
   Would I seek Thy face;
   Heal my wounded, broken spirit,
   Save me by Thy grace.

4. Thou the spring of all my comfort,
   More than life to me!
   Whom have I on earth beside Thee?
   Whom in heav'n but Thee!

Rock of Ages

Text by Augustus M. Toplady
Music by Thomas Hastings

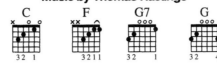

Strum Pattern: 8
Pick Pattern: 8

Additional Lyrics

2. Could my tears forever flow,
   Could my zeal no languor know?
   These for sin could not atone,
   Thou must save and Thou alone.
   I my hand no price I bring,
   Simply to Thy cross I cling.

3. While I draw this fleeting breath,
   When my eyes shall close in death.
   When I rise to worlds unknown,
   And behold Thee on Thy throne.
   Rock of ages cleft for me,
   Let me hide myself in Thee.

Savior Like a Shepherd Lead Us

Traditional

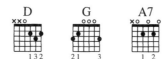

Strum Pattern: 2
Pick Pattern: 2

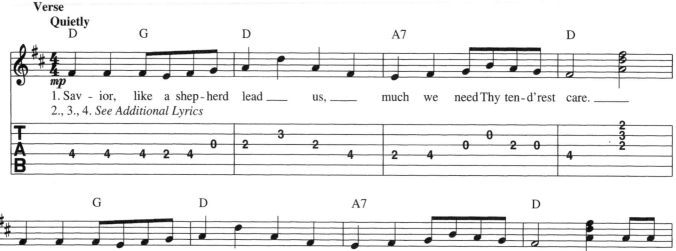

Verse
Quietly

1. Sav - ior, like a shep-herd lead ___ us, ___ much we need Thy ten-d'rest care. ___
2., 3., 4. *See Additional Lyrics*

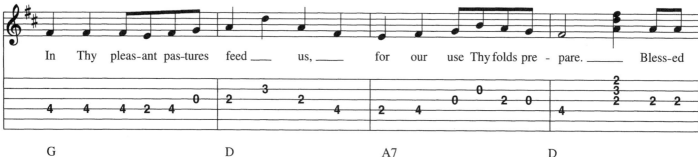

In Thy pleas-ant pas-tures feed ___ us, ___ for our use Thy folds pre - pare. ___ Bless-ed

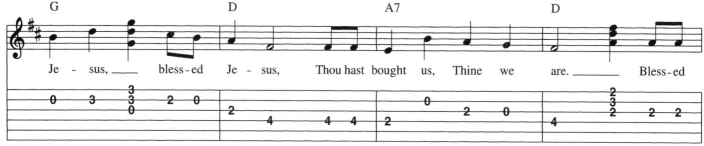

Je - sus, ___ bless-ed Je - sus, Thou hast bought us, Thine we are. ___ Bless-ed

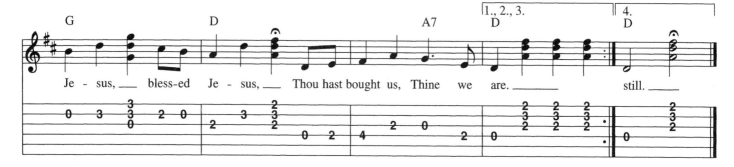

Je - sus, ___ bless-ed Je - sus, ___ Thou hast bought us, Thine we are. ___ still.

Additional Lyrics

2. We are Thine; do Thou befriend us,
   Be the Guardian of our way.
   Keep Thy flock, from sin defend us,
   Seek us when we go astray.
   Blessed Jesus, blessed Jesus,
   Hear, oh hear us when we pray;
   Blessed Jesus, blessed Jesus,
   Hear, oh hear us when we pray.

3. Thou hast promised to receive us,
   Poor and sinful though we be.
   Thou hast mercy to relieve us,
   Grace to cleanse, and pow'r to free.
   Blessed Jesus, blessed Jesus,
   Early let us turn to Thee.
   Blessed Jesus, blessed Jesus,
   Early let us turn to Thee.

4. Early let us seek Thy favor,
   Early let us do Thy will.
   Blessed Lord and only Savior,
   With Thy love our bosoms fill.
   Blessed Jesus, blessed Jesus,
   Thou hast loved us, love us still.
   Blessed Jesus, blessed Jesus,
   Thou hast loved us, love us still.

This Is My Father's World

Words by Maltbie Babcock
Traditional Music

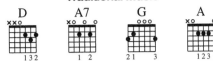

Strum Pattern: 2
Pick Pattern: 2

Additional Lyrics

2. This is my Father's world, the birds their carrols raise.
   The morning light, the lily white, declare their maker's praise.
   This is my Father's world, He shines in all that's fair.
   In the rustling grass I hear Him pass, He speaks to me everywhere.

3. This is my Father's world, oh let me ne'er forget
   That though the wrong seems oft so strong, God is the Ruler yet.
   This is my Father's world, the battle is not done.
   Jesus who died shall be satisfied, and earth and heav'n be one.

Sweet Hour of Prayer

By W.W. Walford and W.B. Bradbury

Strum Pattern: 8
Pick Pattern: 8

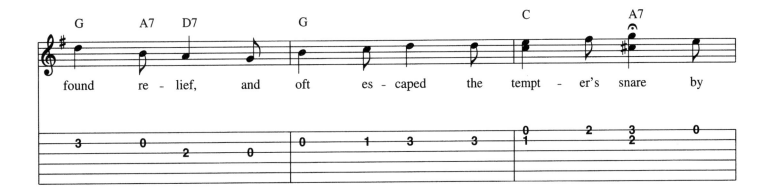

found re - lief, and oft es - caped the tempt - er's snare by

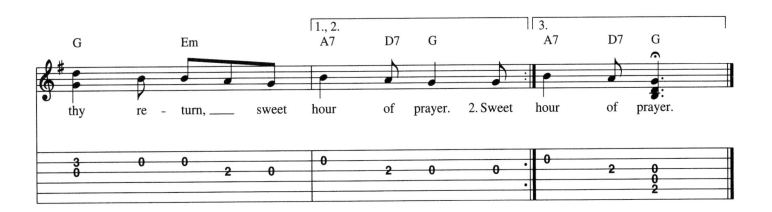

thy re - turn, _____ sweet hour of prayer. 2. Sweet hour of prayer.

Additional Lyrics

2. Sweet hour of prayer,
   Sweet hour of prayer,
   Thy wings shall my petition bear;
   To Him whose truth and faithfulness
   Engage the waiting soul to bless.
   And since He bids me seek His face,
   Believe His word, and trust His grace,
   I'll cast on Him my ev'ry care,
   And wait for thee, sweet hour of prayer.

3. Sweet hour of prayer,
   Sweet hour of prayer,
   May I thy consolation share;
   Till from Mount Pisgah's lofty height
   I view my home and take my flight.
   This robe of flesh I'll drop and rise
   To seize the everlasting prize,
   And shout while passing through the air,
   Farewell, farewell, sweet hour of prayer.

We're Marching to Zion

Traditional

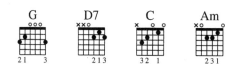

Strum Pattern: 8
Pick Pattern: 8

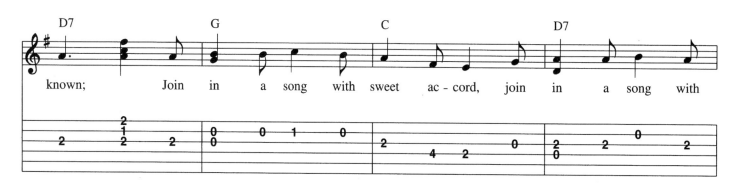

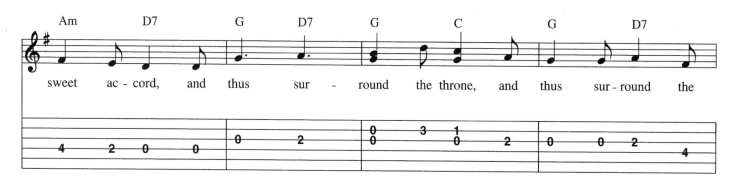

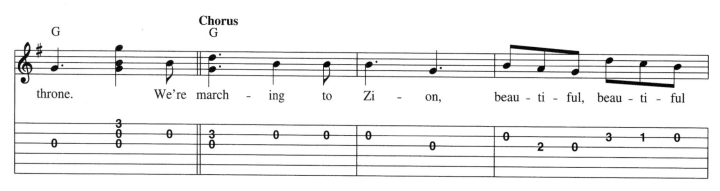

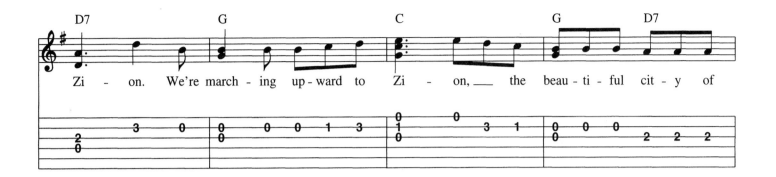

Zi - on. We're march - ing up - ward to Zi - on, ___ the beau - ti - ful cit - y of

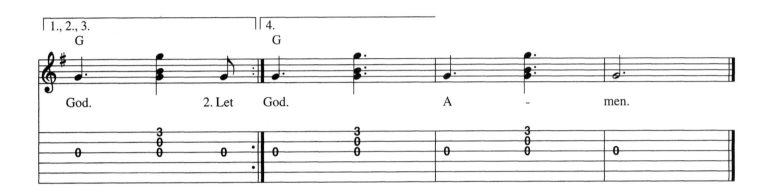

God. 2. Let God. A - men.

Additional Lyrics

2. Let those refuse to sing
   Who never knew our God;
   But children of the heav'nly King,
   But children of the heav'nly King,
   May speak there joys abroad,
   May speak there joys abroad.

3. The hill of Zion yields,
   A thousand sacred sweets,
   Before we reach the heav'nly fields,
   Before we reach the heav'nly fields,
   Or walk the golden streets,
   Or walk the golden streets.

4. Then let our song abound,
   And ev'ry tear be dry;
   We're marching thru Immanuel's ground,
   We're marching thru Immanuel's ground,
   To fairer worlds on high,
   To fairer worlds on high.

Were You There?

Traditional Spiritual

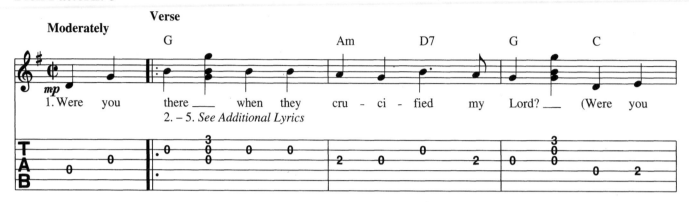

Strum Pattern: 3
Pick Pattern: 3

Moderately

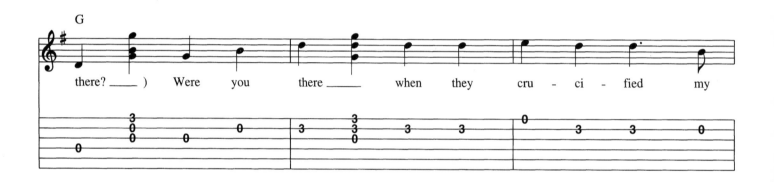

1. Were you there ___ when they cru - ci - fied my Lord? ___ (Were you
2. – 5. *See Additional Lyrics*

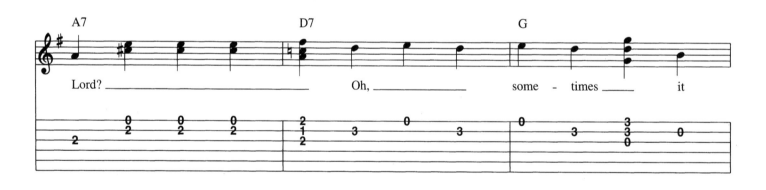

there? ___) Were you there ___ when they cru - ci - fied my

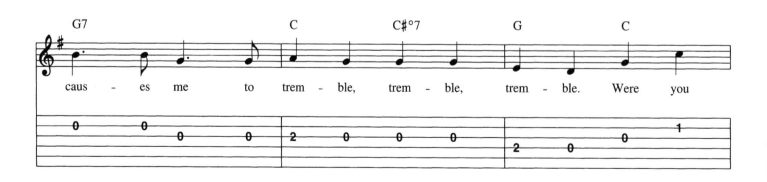

Lord? ___ Oh, ___ some - times ___ it

caus - es me to trem - ble, trem - ble, trem - ble. Were you

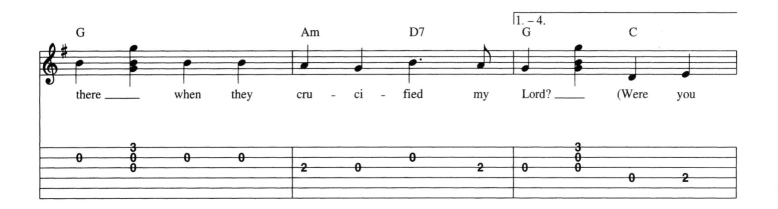

there _____ when they cru - ci - fied my Lord? _____ (Were you

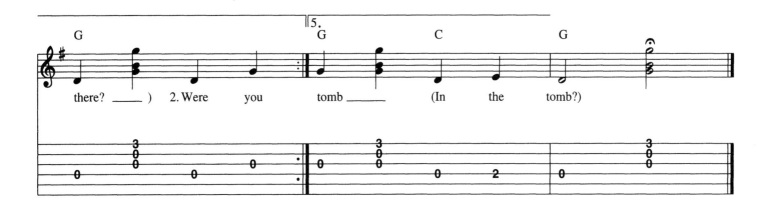

there? _____) 2. Were you tomb _____ (In the tomb?)

Additional Lyrics

2. Were you there when they nailed Him to the tree? (To the tree?)
   Were you there when they nailed Him to the tree? (To the tree?)
   Oh, sometimes it causes me to tremble, tremble, tremble.
   Were you there when they nailed him to the tree? (To the tree?)

3. Were you there when they pierced Him in the side? (In the side?)
   Were you there when they pierced Him in the side? (In the side?)
   Oh, sometimes it causes me to tremble, tremble, tremble.
   Were you there when they pierced Him in the side? (In the side?)

4. Were you there when the sun refused to shine? (Were you there?)
   Were you there when the sun refused to shine? (Were you there?)
   Oh, sometimes it causes me to tremble, tremble, tremble.
   Were you there when the sun refused to shine? (Were you there?)

5. Were you there when they laid Him in the tomb? (In the tomb?)
   Were you there when they laid Him in the tomb? (In the tomb?)
   Oh, sometimes it causes me to tremble, tremble, tremble.
   Were you there when they laid Him in the tomb? (In the tomb?)

What a Friend We Have in Jesus

Words by Joseph Scriven
Music by Charles C. Converse

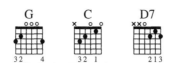

Strum Pattern: 6
Pick Pattern: 4

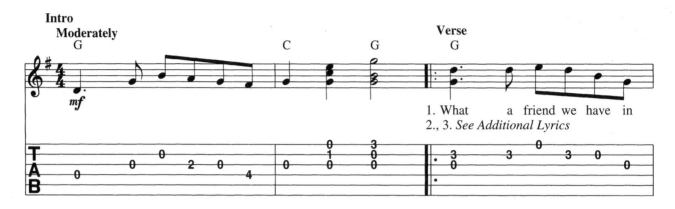

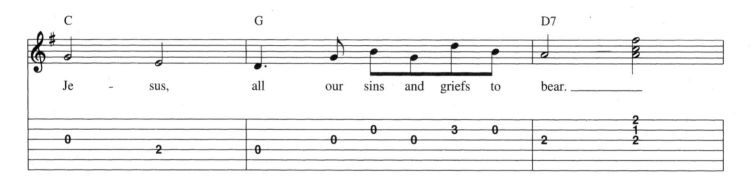

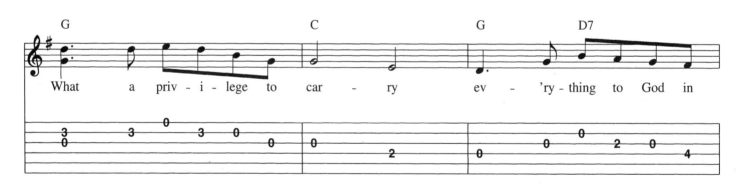

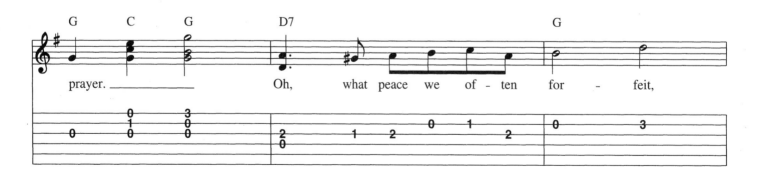

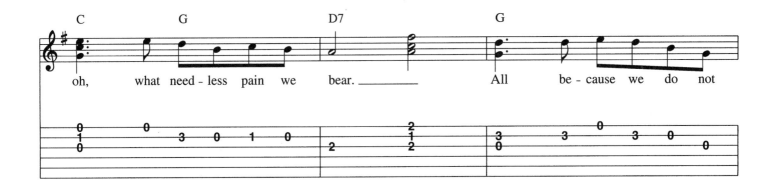

oh, what need - less pain we bear. _____ All be - cause we do not

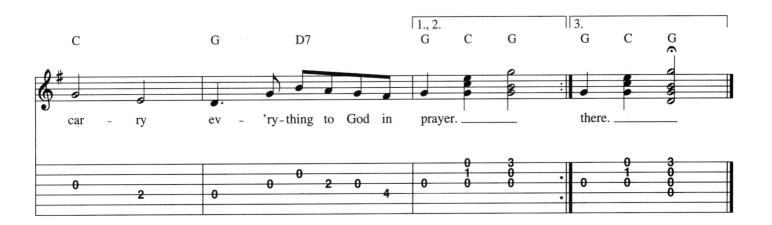

car - ry ev - 'ry-thing to God in prayer. _____ there. _____

Additional Lyrics

2. Have we trials and temptations,
   Is there troubles anywhere?
   We should never be discouraged;
   Take it to the Lord in prayer.
   Can we find a friend so faithful
   Who will all our sorrows share?
   Jesus knows our ev'ry weakness;
   Take it to the Lord in prayer.

3. Are we weak and heavy laden,
   Cumbered with a load of care?
   Precious Savior still our refuge;
   Take it to the Lord in prayer.
   Do thy friends despise, forsake thee?
   Take it to the Lord in prayer.
   In His arms He'll take and shield thee;
   Thou will find a solace there.

Wondrous Love

Southern American Folk Hymn

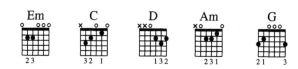

Strum Pattern: 4
Pick Pattern: 6

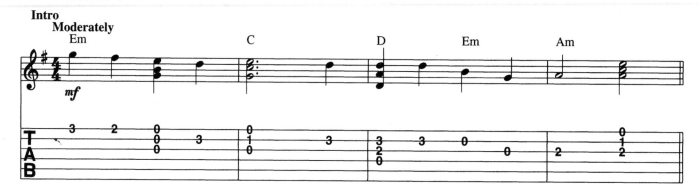

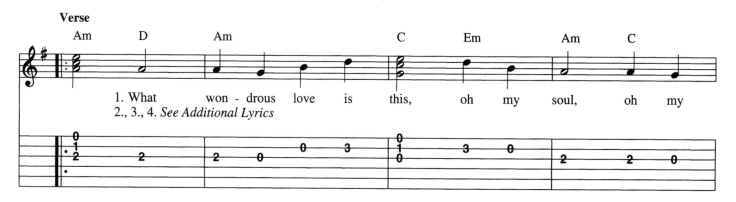

1. What won - drous love is this, oh my soul, oh my
2., 3., 4. *See Additional Lyrics*

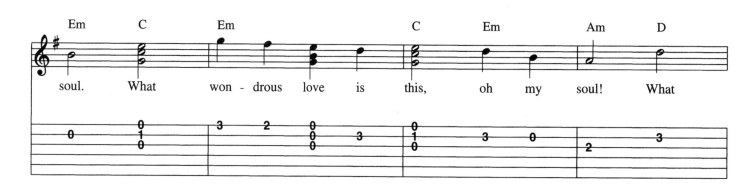

soul. What won - drous love is this, oh my soul! What

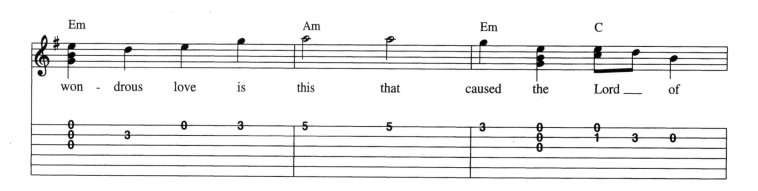

won - drous love is this that caused the Lord ___ of

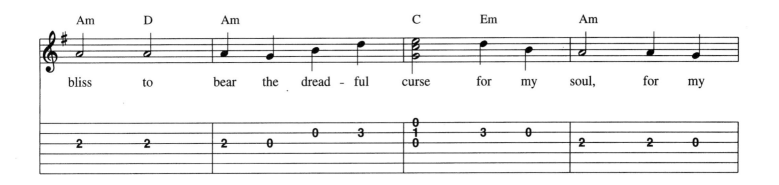

Additional Lyrics

2. What wondrous love is this, oh my soul, oh my soul.
   What wondrous love is this, oh my soul!
   What wondrous love is this that caused the Lord of life
   To lay aside His crown for my soul, for my soul,
   To lay aside His crown for my soul!

3. To God and to the Lamb I will sing, I will sing,
   To God and to the Lamb I will sing.
   To God and to the Lamb who is the great AM,
   While millions join the theme I will sing, I will sing,
   While millions join the theme I will sing.

4. And when from death I'm free, I'll sing on, I'll sing on.
   And when from death I'm free, I'll sing on.
   And when from death I'm free, I'll sing and joyful be,
   And through eternity I'll sing on, I'll sing on,
   And through eternity I'll sing on.

When I Survey the Wondrous Cross

Words by Lowell Mason
Music by Isaac Watts

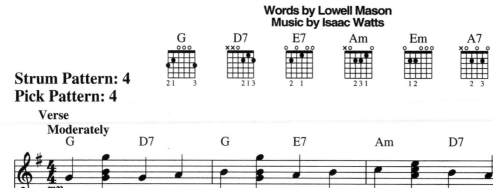

Strum Pattern: 4
Pick Pattern: 4

Verse
Moderately

1. When I sur - vey the won - drous cross
2., 3., 4. *See Additional Lyrics*

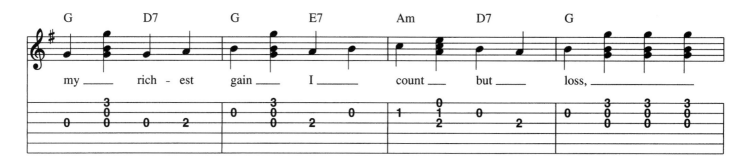

on which the Prince of glo - ry died,

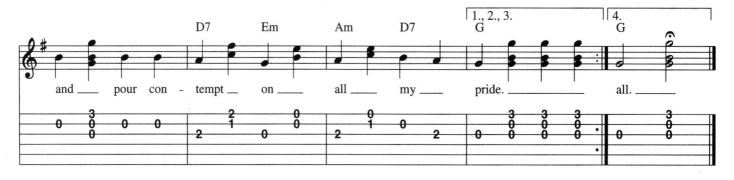

my rich - est gain I count but loss,

and pour con - tempt on all my pride. all.

Additional Lyrics

2. Forbid it, Lord, that I should boast,
Save in the death of Christ, my Lord.
All the vain things that charm me most,
I sacrifice them to His blood.

3. See, from His head, His hands, His feet,
Sorrow and love flow mingled down.
Did e'er such love and sorrow meet
Or thorns compose so rich a crown?

4. Were the whole realm of nature mine,
That were a present far too small.
Love so amazing so divine,
Demands my soul, my life, my all.